Petite Fashion
THE LONG AND SHORT OF IT

Researched and Collated by Sharon Halstead

Copyright © 2018 by Sharon Halstead
Petitepeds® is a registered trademark of Sharon Halstead
All rights reserved, including the right to reproduce this book or portions thereof in any form whatsoever. Affiliate links may be used, which is at not cost to you.

Credits
Cover graphics, book illustrations and Graphic Design by Karen Hue
E-book creation by Luca Funari, lucafunari@hotmail.com
Author and images: Luisa Kearney, ©OnlinePersonalStylist.com, Sharon Halstead © PetitePeds

Contact
Email: sales@petitepeds.com.au
Website AU: www.petitepeds.com.au
Website US: www.petitepeds.co

Melbourne, Australia

Cataloguing
National Library of Australia Cataloguing-in Publication Date
Sharon Halstead's Petite Fashion, the Long and Short of It
Fashion

INTRODUCTION

The Long and Short of it

Petite Fashion

I HAVE A DREAM... a dream to help Petite ladies!

Welcome

The aim of this book is to provide you with numerous tips (sourced, thoroughly researched and then compiled into one easy to read, direct and explicit beautiful book). I am confident it contains quality content to assist all you beautiful petite ladies out there who struggle with dressing your petite frames and feet.

Now in business for a few years, I have heard all the stories of woe and frustration from my petite customers, not just about shoes but clothing and fashion in general. It has been my catch cry that "Dressing a petite lady is different to dressing an average woman, period."

With a firm interest in being the authority on anything petite, I decided to invest in creating a book to dress the unique petite frame, and combined with a qualified fashion stylist so that we could assist our customers. This book is a culmination of all the research, sourced from qualified stylists, customer feedback and good old-fashioned trial and error, into this very unique E-book targeted at petite ladies. As the saying goes, "necessity is the mother of invention" so it was out of a dire need for change that this e-book was born.

Remember this book is essentially a reference book, not to be digested in one sitting, but rather to be referred to whenever you have a fashion dilemma or want to know what goes with what, what will suit your body shape or face shape or skin colour or what accessory to match for your height etc.

I would love to get any feedback so please feel free to contact me with comments, questions or suggestions at

Yours fashionably

Sharron Halstead
Founder, Petitepeds

Contents

CHAPTER 1	Petite Women – what is petite?...	7
CHAPTER 2	Do's and Don'ts...	14
CHAPTER 3	How to create the perfect capsule wardrobe for petite ladies/wardrobe essentials...	21
CHAPTER 4	A mini masterclass on choosing shoes..	27
CHAPTER 5	Dressing for your skin tone..	36
CHAPTER 6	Using colour to dress for your body shape..	44
CHAPTER 7	The Psychology of Color on our Moods, Feelings, and Behaviour	47
CHAPTER 8	Size Guide to Petite Sizes..	50
	How to Measure Your Foot...	55
BIOGRAPHY	....	57
BONUS SECTION	....	58
REVIEW SECTION	....	59
ALSO BY SHARRON HALSTEAD	....	61

CHAPTER 1

Petite woman
what is petite?

Petite is a size determined by nothing more than height

The definition of

adjective:
petite (of a woman) attractively small and dainty.
"she was petite and vivacious"

synonyms:
small, dainty, diminutive, slight, little, tiny, elfin, delicate, small-boned;

It is true

that many petite women have smaller frames and bone structure than non-petite women however, this doesn't mean that all women have delicate face shapes, tiny waists or boyish figures. The standard height of a woman classed as petite is 5 foot 3 or under. Naturally, a woman of 4 ft 11 is going to be significantly shorter and different in shape and body proportions that a woman of 5 ft 3. This is why you need to understand the many aspects of petite dressing.

> On the plus side, petite women can enjoy the luxury of being taller or shorter at any time they choose with the help of a great pair of heels.

There are many advantages to being a *petite lady,* for example:

- Petite women can get away with wearing a greater range of styles and patterns

- Bright colours and different patterns and prints look fabulous on petite women

- It is easier for a petite lady to make herself look curvier, slimmer, taller, younger than her taller counterparts, through the use of clothing.

- Shopping in the sales can (sometimes) be a huge success because we do not share the nation's average shoe and dress size that everybody else seems to be fighting over!

There are four main body shape types:
(we will cover them in more detail throughout this book.)

Apple = you are widest around the tops of your arms, your bust and your waist but are narrower from your hips and below.

Pear = Your widest point is your hips/bottom and thighs - but have a slim, narrow torso.

Straight = Your hips, waist and shoulders all appear the same width and overall, you have a very straight, balanced figure that may appear boyish or athletic.

Hourglass = Your shoulders and bust are approximately the same width as your hips but your waist is around 10 inches smaller. You may also have very slim ankles and wrists.

> The key to dressing well as a petite lady is understanding your body shape and learning how to dress for your own individual body shape, because as we have already established – being petite is not a one size fits all types of body shape.

In order to find

clothing and footwear that suits your height and shape, it is best to make an effort to shop in the petite ranges in stores. It's also very important to pay attention to the type of body shape you have when shopping, as few people actually do this and this is one of the main reasons why all women struggle to find clothing that suits them and that flatters them!

CHAPTER 2

Do's and Don'ts

Common misconceptions about *petite shapes*

There are many misconceptions about the petite figure. Unlike what you may think, petite body shapes do not have to be any of the following:

- "Skinny"
- Underweight
- Petite is a "body shape"
- Petite women are a "one size fits all" kind of community

Another common misconception about petite ladies is that they have a boyish figure and are very thin, but this is not always the case. It's true that usually petite women have smaller frames, which means that their hips and shoulders are narrower than their taller counterparts but some of the most admired and famous hourglass figures belong to petite ladies. Petite ladies do not lack femininity; just merely lack a little height!

> You would be surprised at just how many shorter ladies there are out there, especially if you are comparing yourself to those on the red carpet

Like with all types

of dressing there are certain "do's and don'ts" for shorter ladies too. If you have ever read any kind of media or seen a picture of Hollywood stars on the red carpet then you will see that all of these lovely ladies manage to dress for their shape without looking as though they are drowning in fabric, unlike the petite ladies of the real world! You would be surprised at just how many shorter ladies there are out there, especially if you are comparing yourself to those on the red carpet. With the help of a little extra knowledge and proven style hacks like you will find in this book, it is possible to never have to suffer feeling or looking too short again, just like many of the celebrity ladies out there!

Dos

- Shop in petite ranges to "cheat" your way to tailored fits.

- If you cannot find petite ranges in your nearby clothing stores then hunt out tailor made options.

- In some cases finding decent fitting petite clothing can be a challenge. Rather than buying large quantities of clothing, track down tailor made alternatives and if you have to, invest in a few tailored pieces rather than lots of poor fitting clothing.

- In trousers, straight leg varieties are your best friend. These are the one style that will suit you no matter what your body shape is.

- If possible, match the colour of your footwear to your trousers/bottoms, as this will create the illusion of longer, leaner legs.

- Wear colours from a similar palette, which will complement each other and which will not create a huge contrast. This will make you appear taller, whereas block colours will make you appear shorter.

Here is a list of all the things you should do and all of the things you shouldn't do when dressing your delicate shape.

- Try V-neck tops and ankle length trousers for elongating your torso and legs.
- If you want to elongate the look of your torso opt for longer tops that come to your hip bone or just below.
- If you want to elongate your legs then opt for high waist trousers and skirts.
- Replace wearing chunky belts with skinny belts.
- Wear patterns on the top half of your body to elongate your whole body rather than making your body appear shorter and wider than it is actually is.
- Wear vertical stripes instead of horizontal stripes.
- Wear smaller bags rather than big bags.

 Dont's

- Wearing chunky belts will make you appear shorter than what you are.
- Avoid horizontal stripes which will make you appear shorter and wider.
- Try to avoid larger handbags.
- Don't wear ankle straps on shoes.
- Make sure that your boots do not exceed knee length.
- Don't wear baggy tops and bottoms.
- Don't shop in the kids section.
- Don't go against your natural body shape when dressing and shopping, it will prove a waste of money and time.
- Don't choose bottoms that have an obvious mixture of colour, try to opt for one colour on your bottoms.
- Don't team tunics with leggings and skinny jeans, as this will make your legs look extremely short!
- Don't wear skirts or leggings that come to anywhere between your knee and ankle, opt for leggings and skirts that end either at your knee or ankles but not in between.
- Avoid oversized jewellery and accessories.

CHAPTER 3

How to create

the perfect capsule wardrobe for petite ladies/wardrobe essentials

What is a Capsule Wardrobe?

A capsule wardrobe is a neat and concise wardrobe, full of garments and accessories that suit one another, that can be thrown together with ease to create perfect outfits and also, it must contain items that you will wear regularly. In other words, a capsule wardrobe is a wardrobe full of style staples. One of the biggest mistakes that many women make when dressing, as well as when shopping for clothes, is that they jump into the deep end first and opt for bright colours and daring fits. You must start with the basics, wear them, and gradually build upon them using only items that suit your body shape.

> Start with the basics, wear them, and gradually buil upon them using only itmes that suit your body shape.

the best way

to build a wardrobe that will serve as both useful and fun to work with is to start with the basics and built on what you already have. Ideally, every wardrobe should have a certain number of items from which you will easily be able to form stylish yet fuss free outfits without wasting hours doing so. Of course, feel free to eliminate any items on this list that you just would not wear, but the basics you need to create your perfect capsule wardrobe are:

- Black vest top
- White vest top
- Black t-shirt
- White t-shirt
- Long sleeve black top
- Long sleeve white top
- White blouse
- A basic button up cardigan
- A large scarf/shawl
- A stylish clutch bag
- A big buckle belt
- A cream trench coat
- A black leather jacket
- Black trousers
- Indigo Jeans

- Faded Jeans
- White Jeans
- A well-fitted denim jacket
- A fitted blazer jacket
- A "it fits everything" handbag
- A tailored handbag
- Hoodie type sweatshirt
- Black dress
- A pair of classic stiletto heels
- Silver/gold hoops
- A gold/silver watch
- Pearl earrings (faux or real)
- Shirt dress
- Polo neck top

CHAPTER 4

A mini masterclass on
choosing shoes

what shape/strap/toe shape/style to choose?

As you will probably already know, ladies of 5 ft 3 and under are not all necessarily going to be the Audrey Hepburn's of the world!

However, not surprisingly, some of the most enviable curvaceous and hourglass figures belong to shorter ladies, which is proof that every "body" comes in different shapes and sizes. The most common issue that petite ladies share is finding footwear that neither looks too big for them or too small.

Wearing shoes too small for you can make you appear much larger on the top half of your body, giving you the illusion of incredibly tiny feet and a large upper body even if this is not actually the case. You need to take note of the appearance of a particular pair of shoes around the toe area and note the straps, height and heel too.

Wearing shoes too small for you can make you appear much larger on the top half of your body.

The "tiny foot" problem

You don't have to hunt far to find pictures of women who are no taller than 5 ft 3 who have worn shoes that are too big for their appearance. In the majority of cases, you should avoid bulky looking shoes with a wide, square or rounded toe because they will make your legs appear fuller and shorter, and this could easily knock a few inches off your height.

On the other hand, wearing wide leg trousers, or any garment that has a wide hem anywhere aiming towards your feet, calls for thicker, sturdier looking shoes – something that can carry the look of wide leg trousers on your petite frame.

The look you don't want to create...

Top tip: If you are shopping for footwear and are looking for shoes with a narrow toe but don't want them to make your feet look too tiny and your body out of proportion when wearing them, simply try a pair of pointed toe shoes but with a lower heel, as this will instantly make your feet appear bigger but without losing any of the feminine aspects from the look you were going for

> Open shoes that expose the top part of your foot such as ballet pumps will do a lot of justice for your legs and height

Shoe Rules:

- When wearing bootleg trousers, you should wear wider shoes because pointy heels and narrow shoes will give your body an inverted triangle shape, meaning that your shoulders, bust and waist will seem very broad in comparison with your feet which will appear very small as a result of this poor shoe choice. You should opt for a round or square toe shoe with a thick flat, platform or block heel rather than a stiletto heel.

- When wearing skirts and dresses of any length, other than wearing the look with flip-flops, you should aim to wear daintier shoes, such as pointed toe shoes with smaller, thinner heels. In this case you should avoid ankle straps, thick heels and wide toe shoes.

- Where you can, try to avoid brightly coloured footwear because doing so will shorten and widen the look of your legs and footwear.

- As for boots, try to avoid lengths over the knee or slightly over the ankle. Boots should be ankle boots or knee length but nothing in between or over these specified heights.

- Open shoes that expose the top part of your foot such as ballet pumps will do a lot of justice for your legs and height.

- Ankle straps will "cut off" your legs, making them appear much shorter because that important, delicate 1cm ankle strap is precious room on 29" or below legs. Go for open front shoes in the warmer weather or for formal occasions when possible.

- Ankle boots and shoes with laces at the front will elongate your legs in a balanced way that won't affect the appearance of your legs. On the other hand, zips, tassels and other accessories to the side of shoes and boots (either on the inside of the leg or on the outside of the leg) will add bulk to your legs and could risk you losing definition in your legs.

- In most cases, you should look for boots that are fitted and are not too wide towards the top.

Top tips

When Choosing Shoes:

- Get sized up properly.

- Invest in a few decent pairs that fit you really well. This will save you heaps of time, effort and money in the long-run.

- Be mindful of the types of outfits you will be wearing with your shoes. Make sure that the shoes till look balanced with the outfit you are wearing – see the tips above for more advice on this!

- SHOES NOT TO WEAR

- SHOES TO WEAR

CHAPTER 5

Dressing for your
skin tone

If you have ever been shopping and found that some colours just do not suit your colouring and features, then it is because that colour (or more specifically – that shade of colour) does not suit your skin tone.

In order to find out which colours suit your skin tone, you will need to take into account the natural appearance and colour of the following 4 features:

- Your eye colour
- Your (natural) hair colour
- Your natural eyelash and eyebrow colour
- The appearance of your skin – such as a presence of undertones? Do you have freckles?

How to

Determine Your Skin Tone

Determining what kind of skin tone you have can get very complicated, as there are numerous types of skin tones that are incredibly specific to each person.

Your skin tone may be:
- Clear and cool
- Clear and warm
- Cool and clear
- Cool and soft
- Deep and cool
- Deep and warm
- Light and cool
- Light and warm
- Soft and cool
- Soft and warm
- Warm and clear
- Warm and soft

Determining which of these is your skin tone can get very complicated and is best left to a professional but what you can do is determine whether your skin tone is cool or warm, this of which can easily be done at home and will solve half of your colour-related style issues!

Cool Skin Tones:

- A "cool" skin tone means that you have more ash tones in your hair/eyebrow colour than you do red, auburn and warm brown tones.

- Your skin tone is most likely cool if:

- Your veins on your wrist are blue – not green.

- If your eyes are light/blue or green

- Your natural hair, eyebrow and eyelash colour are dark blonde/light brown to medium brown

Warm Skin Tones:

- A "warm" skin tone means that you have more red/auburn/gold tones in your hair/eyebrow colour than you do ash/non-warm tones.

- Your skin tone is most likely cool if:

- Your veins on your wrist are green – not blue.

- If your eyes are warm/brown/dark blue/green

- Your natural hair, eyebrow and eyelash colour are auburn/light blonde/medium brown to black.

Take the "*Pink test*"

Take a bright pink item of clothing and place it next to your face. Does it bring out the pink in your cheeks in a very flattering way or does it make your whole face look red and blotchy?

Ignore how you feel about the colour pink, just observe how it makes your skin tone look. Is it flattering or unflattering? Does it compliment your skin tone or highlight imperfections?

Cool skin tone

If you have a cool skin tone and/or your skin appears blotchy when doing the above "pink test" then you should stick to cooler colours that balance out any redness in your skin. These colours are often referred to as spring/summer colours because these colour palettes are made up of spring and summer-influenced colours, such as lilac, blue, green, etc.

Here are some examples of colours and tones that would suit you best.

Cool Winter

Cool Summer

Warm skin tone

If you have a warm skin tone and/or the above "pink test" shows off your skin tone in a flattering way then you should opt for warmer colours that bring out your rosy cheeks that are often disguised by your warmer, olive-type complexion.

These colours are often referred to as autumn/winter colours because these colour palettes are made up of autumn and winter-influenced colours, such as burgundy, orange, emerald green, etc.

Here are some examples of colours and tones that would suit you best.

Warm Spring

Warm Autumn

CHAPTER 6

Using colour to dress for your
body shape

Mixing Colours Well

The reason so many people struggle with matching different colours that go well together is because they are choosing from a much larger colour range, rather than choosing from the colour palette suited to their own personal skin tone. Once you know which colours truly suit you, you can mix and match any of these colours and they will instantly compliment your skin tone & features, and these colours chosen will also complement each other too because they will be from a similar colour palette.

Creating Colour Confidence

The key to dressing well and feeling great is to wear and buy 80% of styles and colours that suit you and 20% of things that you love too much to care how much they suit you. There will be colours that are supposed to suit your skin tone well but just because they suit your skin tone it doesn't mean that you are guaranteed to like them and that's ok. If you do not like a particular colour, you don't feel confident in it or perhaps it makes you feel depressed then simply don't wear it - you don't have to! Stick to colours that you like but work out the best way to wear them first! You may prefer some colours in the form of an accessory such as a handbag, necklace, scarf, pair of earrings, etc. If you want to become more daring with colour, either take the plunge and wear the colours that you have not yet dared to wear or make the process a gradual one by choosing a smaller item or an accessory in that shade at first so that you get used to seeing that colour on you.

CHAPTER 7

The Psychology of *Colour* on our Moods, Feelings and Behaviour

The Psychology of Colour on our Moods, Feelings and Behaviour

Cool Colours

Colour is a powerful force in our lives and can have a profound effect on our bodies and minds.

Colours in the blue side of the spectrum are known as cool colours and can invoke feelings ranging from calm to sadness or indifference.

See our chart beside on the possible effects on your mood as well as possible reactions of others depending on the colour you choose to wear.

Dark Green #2b5846
Restful, hushed, reliable, prosperity, stately, trustworthy

Follage Greens #39754a
Fertile, healthy, growth, soothing, harmony, restful, restoration

Bright Green #49a368
Fresh, grass, Irish, lively, spring, renewal, lush

Emerald #4aa28c
Luxurious, jewel-like, up-scale, ritzy, expensive

Aqua #b5dcd3
Aware, refreshing, cleansing, young and dreamy, lighthearted

Turquoise #7bc7bd
Infinity, compassionate, protective, faithful, tropical

Teal #337c91
Serene, cool, tasteful, sophisticated, confident

Sky Blue #93bdcd
Heavenly, true, dependable, restful, tranquil, open, reassuring

Light Blue #afcbe4
Calm, quiet, patient, peaceful, cool, water, clean

Periwinkle #93a7d3
Genial, lively, sprightly, convivial, cordial

Bright Blue #3889c2
Electric, brisk, vibrant, energy, stirring, impressive, exhilarating

Deep Blue #343f79
Credible, authoritative, basic, conservative, strong, reliable

Lavender #ba66a3
Romantic, nostalgic, fanciful, lightweight, lightly scented

Mauve #ab8da0
Wistful, sentimental, thoughtful, compassionate

Amethyst #co9ec2
Curative, protective, peace of mind, calming

Blue Purple #74519b
Contemplative, meditative, spiritual, mysterious, enchanting

Red Purple #8b4f9f
Sensual, thrilling, witty, intensely exciting, dramatic, expressive

Deep Purple #4a2d5b
Visionary, rich, royal, prestigious, subduing, distant, introspective

Neutral Grey #9c9c9d
Classic, sober, corporate, timeless, quiet, logical, deliberate

Charcoal Grey #696c6f
Steadfast, responsible, staunch, accountable, enduring

Taupe #b7b29d
Practical, timeless, authentic, organic, versatile, understated

Ivory #f6f0d8
Soft, subtle, cozy, dusky, gentle, composed, nostalgic

Silver (Metallic)
Sleek, classy, stylish, modern, cool, smooth

Black #000000
Empowered, elegant, mysterious, sophisticated, bold, classic, sober

White #ffffff
Pure, clean, pristine, virginal, spotless, innocent, silent, airy

Warm Colours

The Psychology of Colour on our Moods, Feelings and Behaviour

> Colour is a powerful force in our lives and can have a profound effect on our bodies and minds.
>
> Colours in the red area of the colour spectrum are known as warm colours and can evoke emotions ranging from warmth and comfort to anger and hostility.
>
> See our chart below on the possible effects on your mood as well as possible reactions of others depending on the colour you choose to wear.

Deep Red #ad4157
Rich, elegant, refined, tasty, expensive, mature, sumptuous

Brick Red #7e3b40
Earthy, warm, strong, sturdy, established, country

Bright Red #ca4747
Exciting, energizing, passionate, powerful, dynamic, sexy, assertive

Bright Pink #e0698d
Theatrical, playful, high-energy, sensual, wild, tropical, flirty

Dusty Pink #dab6be
Soft, subtle, cozy, dusky, gentle, composed, nostalgic

Light Pink #f3c8d6
Romantic, affectionate, soft, tender, delicate, innocent, fragile

Peach #f5ecba
Nurturing, fuzzy, tactile, centered, comforting, calming, soothing

Coral #e99d8d
Life force, energizing, flexibility, desires, comforting

Tangerine #eda45c
Vital, juice, fruitful, energizing, tangy, youthful

Vibrant Orange #e6B751
Fun, whimsical, childlike, happy, active, glowing, friendly, expansive, jovial

Ginger #c45950
Spicy, flavorful, tangy, pungent, exotic, hot

Terra Cotta #bd826f
Earthy, country, wholesome, welcoming, abundance, warm

Tan #c0946e
Rugged, outdoor, rustic, woodsy, grounded

Chocolate Brown #734d3e
Delicious, rich, appetizing, robust, mouth watering

Earth Brown #6a5c56
Steady, solid, rooted, sheltering, warm, durable, secure, reliable

Gold (Metallic)
Bling, rich, divine, intuitive, luxurious, opulent, valuable, radiant

Amber #d39252
Jewelry, multi-cultural, mellow, abundant, original, autumn

Golden Yellow #eeb959
Nourishing, buttery, tasty, sun-baked, comfort, hospitable

Bright Yellow #f9d65c
Joyful, illuminating, alert, friendly, energetic, innovative, surprise

Light Yellow #f4e251
Cheering, happy, soft, sunny, warming, sweet, easy, pleasing

Chartreuse #e0ad80
Artsy, bold, trendy, startling, sharp, pungent

Light Green #c3d9a9
Calm, quiet, soothing, balanced, neutral

Olive Green #919e67
Military, camouflage, safari, classic, outdoorsy

Lime #93a762
Fresh, citrusy, youthful, acidic, tart, refreshing

CHAPTER 8 Size Guide to
Petite sizes

International Clothing Size Guide

Petite = 5 ft 3 and under

Euro size	Australia size	UK size	Length (CM)	Circumference (CM)
35	1	2	233.31	234.5
36	2	3	239.98	239.0
37	3	4	246.65	243.5
38	4	5	253.32	248.0

UK Sizes (inches)	XS (6)	S (8-10)	M (12-14)	L (16-18)	XL (20-22)	XXL (24-26)
Bust	33"	34-35"	36-37"	$38^{1/2}$-40"	$41^{1/2}$-$43^{1/2}$"	$45^{1/2}$-$47^{1/2}$"
Waist	25"	26-27"	28-29"	$30^{1/2}$-32"	$33^{1/2}$-$35^{1/2}$"	$37^{1/2}$-$39^{1/2}$"
Hips	35"	36-37"	38-39"	$40^{1/2}$-42"	$43^{1/2}$-$45^{1/2}$"	$47^{1/2}$-$49^{1/2}$"
Arm length (petite)	29"	$29^{1/4}$ - $29^{1/2}$"	$29^{3/4}$ – 30"	$30^{1/4}$-$30^{1/2}$"	$30^{3/4}$-$30^{7/8}$"	$33^{7/8}$-34"

International Bra Sizes & Guide

A common issue among ladies with small bone structure is that they require a small band size in their bra but need a larger cup size. For e.g. you may try a bra that's a UK size 34A but find that the band is too large for the size of your back but the cup fits fine. In this case you need to go down a band size and up a cup size – this is a handy trick to know if you do not have the opportunity to go for a professional bra fitting or in the case that a bra you've tried doesn't fit the same way that others in that size do.

Here below is the full list of "petite bra sizes" and their international size equivalents.

AUSTRALIA / NZ	USA	UK / INDIA	EUROPA / CHINA / JAPAN / HONG KONG / KOREA	FRANCE / SPAIN / BELGIUM
8AA	30AA	30A	65A	80A
8A	30A	30B	65B	80B
8B	30B	30C	65C	80C
8C	30C	30D	65D	80D
8D	30D	30DD	65E	80E
8DD	30DD	30E	65F	80F
10AA	32AA	32A	70A	85A
10A	32A	32B	70B	85B
10B	32B	32C	70C	85C
10C	32C	32D	70D	85D
10D	32D	32DD	70E	85E
10DD	32DD	32E	70F	85F

AUSTRALIA / NZ	USA	UK / INDIA	EUROPA / CHINA / JAPAN / HONG KONG / KOREA	FRANCE / SPAIN BELGIUM	AUSTRALIA / NZ	USA	UK / INDIA	EUROPA / CHINA / JAPAN / HONG KONG / KOREA	FRANCE / SPAIN BELGIUM
10E	32DDD/F	32F	70G	85G	14F	36F	36G	80H	95H
10F	32F	32G	70H	85H	14G	36G	36H	80I	95I
10G	32G	32H	70I	85I					
12AA	34AA	34A	75A	90A					
12A	34A	34B	75B	90B					
12B	34B	34C	75C	90C					
12C	34C	34D	75D	90D					
12D	34D	34DD	75E	90E					
12DD	34DD	34E	75F	90F					
12E	34DDD/E	34F	75G	90G					
12F	34F	34G	75H	90H					
12G	34G	34H	75I	90I					
14A	36A	36B	80B	95B					

Shoe Size Conversion Chart

A combination of Foot Length, Width and Arch comprises a person's exact shoe size. Example if 2 people have the same foot length but their width and arch is different they WILL wear different size shoes.

Australia	US	Europe	UK	Asia	China	Foot Length (cm)	Foot Width (Girth) cm	Foot Arch (cm)
1	2	32	13	210	32	18-20	20	21
2	3	33	1	215	33	19-20	21	21
2.5	4	34	1.5	220	34	19-20	22	23
3	4.5	34.5	2	225	34.5	21.5		
3.5	5	35	2.5	230	35	22.8		
4	5.5	36	3	235	36	23.1		
4.5	6	37	3.5	240	37	23.5		

Components of Petite Peds Shoes

upper — lining — sole — leather — coatd — textile — other material

How to find your size

Foot Girth
- Measure in bare foot
- Measure the widest part of each foot

Foot Length
- Measure in bare foot
- Straight-line from bottom line to top

Foot Arch
Measure in Barefoot
Measure around the arch of the foot

www.petitepeds.com

Biography

Sharron Halstead is the Founder of Petitepeds, a global online shoe store catering exclusively to ladies with petite feet.

After receiving a multitude of enquiries, comments, complaints, expletives from customers who were fed-up of being treated like second class citizens by the fashion houses, Sharron and her team went about writing "Petite Fashion – The Long and Short of It" to help petite ladies find their own style and sass, and not be at the mercy of a fashion retail world catering primarily to the average size body and foot, but rather use their unique advantage to get the best out of it.

From humble beginnings out of her garage in Melbourne, Australia, she has spread her wings into global markets to assist all petite ladies, the world over, find themselves, their confidence and their self esteem by learning about the basics on how to dress their unique body shapes and petite feet.

Dear Petite Lady,

As a thank you for purchasing this book, I'd like to give you a **FREE E-Book** specifically written to help you on your journey in transforming your Personal Style and Image.

Please visit

http://bit.ly/petitepeds
to claim your FREE Copy
TODAY!

Dear Petite Lady,

hope you enjoyed reading this book as much as I enjoyed putting it together for you. As you can see it is not a book that you read once, but more of a reference library for all things Style for the Petite Lady.

If you enjoyed the book and found it useful, I'd be very grateful if you would post an honest review on our Amazon Page as well as on our Google and Facebook Page.

Your support really does matter and will make a difference, not only to us but also to the countless Petite ladies who want to purchase the book.

I do read all the reviews so I can get your feedback in real time.

Here are the links to leave reviews:

Facebook Review	http://bit.ly/PetitepedsFB
Google Review	http://bit.ly/PetitepedsGoogle
Amazon Review	http://bit.ly/PetiteFashion1

Thank you for your Support!

Yours fashionably

Sharron
Founder, PetitePeds

www.ingramcontent.com/pod-product-compliance
Lightning Source LLC
Chambersburg PA
CBHW061759290426
44109CB00030B/2893